# Mental Maths Ages

**Anita Straker**

CAMBRIDGE
UNIVERSITY PRESS

## 1a

1. Add 3 and 5.
2. 7 take away 2.
3. 4 + 4.
4. Half of 10.
5. 4 × 2.
6. Which is more: 7 or 8?
7. 9 − 3.
8. 6 ÷ 2.
9. Write **fourteen** in figures.
10. Eight minus five.

## 1b

1. Ella had 2 sweets in one hand and 4 in the other.
   How many sweets did she have?

2. Which is even: 4, 7 or 9?

3. What shape comes next?

4. How many days is one week?

5. I knocked down 3 of my 10 skittles.
   How many were left standing?

6. What is next: 2, 4, 6, 8 …?

7. How much is this
   altogether?

8. Dad gave Sam 4p.  Mum gave him 3p.
   How much was he given?

9. There were 6 cakes for tea.  4 were eaten.
   How many were left?

10. It is 2 o'clock.  How many hours to 5 o'clock?

Here are six rows of letters.

| | | | | | | | |
|---|---|---|---|---|---|---|---|
| Row 1 | A | N | R | Z | P | L | M |
| Row 2 | B | O | X | H | J | D | E |
| Row 3 | F | T | W | N | C | Q | H |
| Row 4 | D | S | A | B | G | D | Y |
| Row 5 | E | Z | V | A | S | E | R |
| Row 6 | U | N | K | C | I | F | J |

Write these.

1  The second letter of the fourth row.
2  The sixth letter of the third row.
3  The first letter of the sixth row.
4  The fourth letter of the fifth row.
5  The third letter of the first row.
6  The seventh letter of the second row.

Now draw the shape whose name you found.

1  Find the sum of 1 and 9.
2  $8 \div 2$.
3  Write **twelve** in figures.
4  Two threes.
5  $4 - 2$.

6  Which is fewer: 3 dots or 4 dots?
7  $2 + 6$.
8  Two more than three.
9  $7 \times 1$.
10  Subtract 1 from 4.

## 2a

**1** What time is it?

**2** It is March. What is next month?

**3** Jo is 8 years old. How old was she two years ago?

**4** Is the seventh box from the left black or white?

**5** My sweets cost 8p. How much change did I get from 10p?

**6** Is 13 odd or even?

**7** What shape is outside all the others?

**8** Mary has 9 marbles. Kate has 4.
How many more has Mary than Kate?

**9** Aziz ate 4 of his 8 toffees. How many did he have left?

**10** The sum of two numbers is 9. One number is 6.
What is the other?

## 2b

**1** $5 + \square = 9$.

**2** Increase 3 by 2.

**3** $6 \div 3$.

**4** What is next: 1, 3, 5, 7 ...?

**5** $3 + 5$.

**6** Which is less: 6 cm or 9 cm?

**7** Write **nineteen** in figures.

**8** $7 - 6$.

**9** $5 \times 2$.

**10** Which two coins make 7p?

1 Two less than five.

2 $3 + 7$.

3 Two fives.

4 $6 - 4$.

5 Is 16 odd or even?

6 Write **twenty** in figures.

7 $\square + 2 = 8$.

8 $1 \times 9$.

9 Decrease 7 by 5.

10 $9 \div 3$.

**2d**

Copy the diagram.

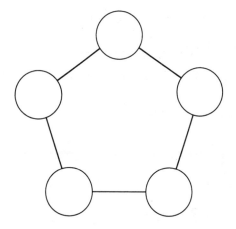

Use each of the numbers 1 to 5.
Write a number in every circle.

Numbers joined by lines must
differ by more than 1.

Now try this one.

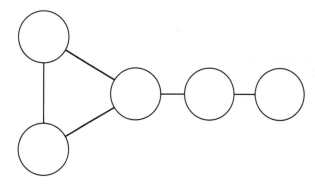

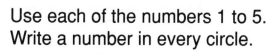

## 3a

1 Write **eleven** in figures.

2 How many corners in a rectangle?

3 Which two coins make 10p?

4 How many hours from 2 o'clock to 4 o'clock?

5 Is the tenth box from the right black or white?

6 How many toes on two feet?

7 How much more is 10p than 6p?

8 It is Wednesday.  What is tomorrow?

9 Which two add up to eight: 3, 4, 5?

10 I ate 7 of my 10 apples.  How many were left?

## 3b

1 Who is the youngest?

2 Who is one year older than Carol?

3 Who was 4 one year ago?

4 Who will be 8 next birthday?

5 Who was 7 two years ago?

6 How much older is Ian than Ann?

7 Who will be 10 in two years' time?

8 Who is older than Lisa?

9 How long will it be before Carol is 10?

10 How old was Lisa 5 years ago?

**Today's birthdays.**

| Name | Age |
|------|-----|
| Ian | 8 |
| Carol | 7 |
| Lisa | 9 |
| Martin | 6 |
| Ram | 10 |
| Ann | 5 |
| Kelly | 4 |

## 3c

1.  Which is odd: 11, 12 or 16?

2.  Today is Sunday.  What was yesterday?

3.  What is next: 0, 3, 6, 9 …?

4.  Is 8 nearer to 5 or nearer to 10?

5.  It is 10 o'clock.  What time was it 2 hours ago?

6.  From the left, what position is the fourth white bead?

7.  2 cakes fit in a box.
How many boxes are needed for 5 cakes?

8.  What shape comes next?

9.  Find the difference between 3 and 8.

10.  How many socks in 3 pairs?

## 3d

Copy the diagram.
Write the numbers from 1 to 5 in the circles.

Each line must have the same total.
Do it in three different ways.

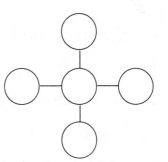

## 4a

1   Find the sum of 3 and 6.
2   $0 \times 4$.
3   Two fours.
4   $9 - 2$.
5   Share 9 between 3.
6   Write **forty-two** in figures.
7   Which is more: 13 kg or 15 kg?
8   $4 + 3$.
9   Four less than ten.
10   $10 \div 2$.

## 4b

1   What is the first month of the year?
2   What time was 3 hours before 8 o'clock?
3   How many sides has a triangle?
4   How many centimetres in a metre?
5   What is next: 1, 4, 7, 10 …?
6   Put in order, smallest first: 32, 17, 23, 71.
7   How many days from Sunday to Friday?
8   What is next: 11, 9, 7, 5 …?
9   Which three coins make 6p?
10   What colour is the 11th bead from the right?

## 4c

1   Subtract 7 from 10.
2   $2 + 2 + 2$.
3   Write **sixty** in figures.
4   Four plus six.
5   Two multiplied by three.
6   What is the month after May?
7   $4 \times 3$.
8   Divide ten by five.
9   $4 \div 2$.
10   $\square - 2 = 6$.

# At the sweet shop

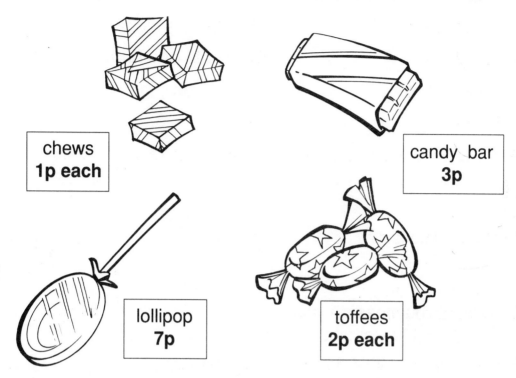

chews
**1p each**

candy bar
**3p**

lollipop
**7p**

toffees
**2p each**

1    What is the cost of three toffees?

2    How much altogether are two chews and a lollipop?

3    Which costs more: a lollipop or two candy bars?

4    What is the cost of two toffees, one candy bar and a chew?

5    How much more is a lollipop than a toffee?

6    How much change from 5p do you get for a candy bar?

7    How many toffees can you buy for 10p?

8    Jenny has saved 2p towards a lollipop.
     How much more must she save?

9    Which two coins will buy you a lollipop?

10   Which two coins will buy you eight chews and a toffee?

## 5a

| | | | |
|---|---|---|---|
| **1** | $10 \div 1$. | **6** | Which is more: 16 or 61? |
| **2** | Increase 9 by 1. | **7** | $2 + 7$. |
| **3** | $2 \times 2$. | **8** | Write **one hundred** in figures. |
| **4** | Divide 8 by 4. | **9** | $10 - 6$. |
| **5** | $\square + 5 = 10$. | **10** | $3 + 3 + 3$. |

## 5b

**1**    What time is it?

**2**    Would you measure your height in litres or centimetres?

**3**    It is Friday. What day was it two days ago?

**4**    How many months in a year?

**5**    What is the least number of coins needed to make 9p?

**6**    Make the biggest number you can with these digits.

 2 3 4

**7**    What is next: 12, 9, 6, 3 ...?

**8**    What must you multiply 2 by to make 14?

**9**    What is one less than 37?

**10**    What shape is inside all the others?

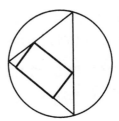

Use these dominoes.

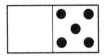 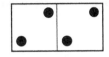 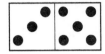 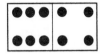

Copy this square.

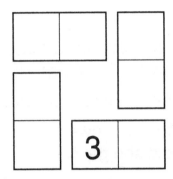

Write the number of domino spots in the boxes.

Each side of the square must add up to 10.

Touching numbers do not need to match.

| | | | |
|---|---|---|---|
| **1** | Decrease 8 by 4. | **6** | $3 \times 3$. |
| **2** | $5 + 4$. | **7** | Which 3 coins make 5p? |
| **3** | Which is less: 12 or 21? | **8** | $5 \times 0$. |
| **4** | Half of 6. | **9** | $9 - 4$. |
| **5** | $2 \div 2$. | **10** | Two sixes. |

## 6a

1. How many corners has a triangle?
2. How many months from June to October?
3. Would you weigh yourself in kilograms or kilometres?
4. Which three coins make 8p?
5. What fraction of this circle is shaded?

6. Jane had 5 conkers and Simon had 9.
   They gave them all to Ali. How many has Ali?
7. How long is it from half past one to half past two?
8. Alice paid 20p for four 1p chews.
   How much change did she get?

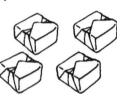

9. How many days is Thursday from last Sunday?
10. There are 12 apples in a basket.
    6 are bad. How many are good?

## 6b

1. Half of 20p.
2. Subtract 7 from 17.
3. Six twos.
4. Add 5 and 6.
5. From 13 take away 9.
6. Which two add to ten: 6, 3, 4?
7. 6p plus 9p.
8. Find the product of 4 and 3.
9. What is next: 18, 16, 14, 12 ...?
10. Which is greater: 37 or 73?

In this 2 × 2 square the numbers add up to 10.

| 1 | 3 |
|---|---|
| 4 | 2 |

Copy and complete these two grids.

**a.** Make each 2 × 2 square add up to 10.

| 4 | 2 | 5 | 1 |
|---|---|---|---|
| 3 |   |   |   |
| 3 |   |   |   |
| 1 |   |   |   |

**b.** Make each 2 × 2 square add up to 12.

| 2 | 1 | 6 | 1 |
|---|---|---|---|
| 7 |   |   |   |
| 2 |   |   |   |
| 7 |   |   |   |

**1** $2 \times \square = 12$.

**2** Three fours.

**3** $7 + 7$.

**4** Half of eight.

**5** $6 + 4 - 7$.

**6** What is next: 19, 17, 15, 13 …?

**7** $18 \div 2$.

**8** $14 - 11$.

**9** Which is less: 16 or 26?

**10** One more than 99.

## 7a

1  Double six.

2  Is 14 nearer to 10 or 20?

3  How many hours in a day?

4  10 + 3.

5  Ten tens.

6  16 ÷ 2.

7  Half of 8 kg.

8  15 − 6.

9  $\square \times 7 = 14$.

10  What is the value of 2 in 27?

## 7b

1  What is this shape called?

2  What is four days after Tuesday?

3  What is the least number of coins needed to make 14p?

4  Which divides exactly by three: 12, 13 or 14?

5  What unit would you use to measure the length of a pencil?

6  What is next: 2, 5, 8, 11 …?

7  Dan has four 2p coins.
   He gives half of them to Sarah.  How much does she get?

8  Two girls have 7 books each.
   How many books do they have altogether?

9  It is November.  How many months ago was June?

10  How many triangles can you see altogether?

## 7c

| | | | |
|---|---|---|---|
| **1** | How many tens in 48? | **6** | $\square \div 5 = 2$. |
| **2** | Double thirty. | **7** | What are the weekend days? |
| **3** | Decrease 10 by 3. | **8** | 7 times 10. |
| **4** | Is 16 nearer 10 or 20? | **9** | $9 + 5$. |
| **5** | $12 - 4$. | **10** | Round 23 to the nearest 10. |

## 7d

Draw two rings.

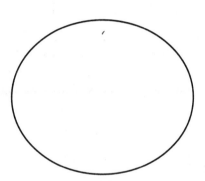 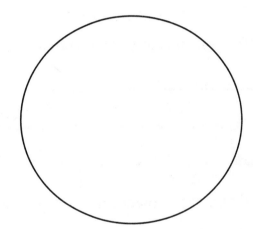

Use each number from 1 to 5 once.
Write them in the rings.

The sum of the numbers in one ring must be twice
the sum of the numbers in the other ring.

Do it in three different ways.

1 2 3 4 5

## 8a

1  What is two days before Sunday?

2  2 children can sit at a table. How many can sit at 9 tables?

3  How many corners has a square?

4  Which three coins make 20p?

5  Do your shoes weigh nearer 1 kg or 10 kg?

6  How many halves make one whole?

7  Which two differ by five: 8, 13, 19?

8  Which divides exactly by four: 14, 15 or 16?

9  What is three months after November?

10  What numbers are missing: 16, 13, 10, 7, □, □ ?

## 8b

Copy the crossword on squared paper.

Write the answers in words: ONE, TWO, THREE …

**Across**

1.  $9 - 7$

3.  $2 + 4$

4.  $6 \times 2$

5.  $11 - 2$

**Down**

2.  $5 + 4 - 8$

3.  $14 \div 2$

4.  $12 - 5 + 3$

# Mental Maths Ages 7–8 Answers

This book covers:
- addition and subtraction facts to 10/20 and beyond
- multiplication and division in the range 0 to 20, and by 10 up to 10 x 10
- rounding to the nearest 10
- splitting numbers into tens and units
- odd and even numbers
- halves and quarters
- telling the time (o'clock and half-past)
- days of the week and months of the year
- use of coins to 20p
- cm, m, kg, litres
- 2D shapes

## Task 1a
1  8
2  5
3  8
4  5
5  8
6  8
7  6
8  3
9  14
10  3

## Task 1b
1  6 sweets
2  4 is even
3  White triangle
4  7 days
5  7 skittles
6  10
7  9p
8  7p
9  2 cakes
10  3 hours

## Task 1c
1  S
2  Q
3  U
4  A
5  R
6  E

## Task 1d
1  10
2  4
3  12
4  6
5  2
6  3 dots
7  8
8  5
9  7
10  3

## Task 2a
1  4 o'clock
2  April
3  6 years old
4  Black
5  2p
6  13 is odd
7  The square
8  5 marbles
9  4 toffees
10  3

## Task 2b
1  4
2  5
3  2
4  9
5  8
6  6 cm is less
7  19
8  1
9  10
10  5p and 2p

## Task 2c
1  3
2  10
3  10
4  2
5  16 is even
6  20
7  6
8  9
9  2
10  3

## Task 2d
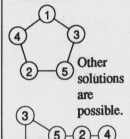
Other solutions are possible.

## Task 3a
1  11
2  4 corners
3  5p and 5p
4  2 hours
5  Black
6  10 toes
7  4p more
8  Thursday
9  3 and 5
10  3 apples

## Task 3b
1  Kelly
2  Ian
3  Ann
4  Carol
5  Lisa
6  3 years
7  Ian
8  Ram
9  3 years
10  4 years old

## Task 3c
1  11 is odd
2  Saturday
3  12
4  Nearer to 10
5  8 o'clock
6  Ninth
7  3 boxes
8  Shaded circle
9  5
10  6 socks

## Task 3d

## Task 4a

1. 9
2. 0
3. 8
4. 7
5. 3
6. 42
7. 15 kg is more
8. 7
9. 6
10. 5

## Task 4b

1. January
2. 5 o'clock
3. 3 sides
4. 100 cm
5. 13
6. 17, 23, 32, 71
7. 5 days
8. 3
9. 2p, 2p, 2p
10. White

## Task 4c

1. 3
2. 6
3. 60
4. 10
5. 6
6. June
7. 12
8. 2
9. 2
10. 8

## Task 4d

1. 6p
2. 9p
3. A lollipop
4. 8p
5. 5p
6. 2p
7. 5 toffees
8. 5p
9. 5p and 2p
10. 5p and 5p

## Task 5a

1. 10
2. 10
3. 4
4. 2
5. 5
6. 61 is more
7. 9
8. 100
9. 4
10. 9

## Task 5b

1. Half past 8
2. Centimetres
3. Wednesday
4. 12 months
5. Three coins
6. 432
7. 0
8. 7
9. 36
10. A rectangle

## Task 5c

| 6 | 4 | 0 |
|---|---|---|
| 2 |   | 5 |
| 2 | 3 | 5 |

## Task 5d

1. 4
2. 9
3. 12 is less
4. 3
5. 1
6. 9
7. 2p, 2p, 1p
8. 0
9. 5
10. 12

## Task 6a

1. 3 corners
2. 4 months
3. Kilograms
4. 5p, 2p, 1p
5. Half
6. 14 conkers
7. 1 hr (60 mins)
8. 16p
9. 4 days
10. 6 apples

## Task 6b

1. 10p
2. 10
3. 12
4. 11
5. 4
6. 6 and 4
7. 15p
8. 12
9. 10
10. 73 is greater

## Task 6c

a.

| 4 | 2 | 5 | 1 |
|---|---|---|---|
| 3 | 1 | 2 | 2 |
| 3 | 3 | 4 | 2 |
| 1 | 3 | 0 | 4 |

b.

| 2 | 1 | 6 | 1 |
|---|---|---|---|
| 7 | 2 | 3 | 2 |
| 2 | 1 | 6 | 1 |
| 7 | 2 | 3 | 2 |

## Task 6d

1. 6
2. 12
3. 14
4. 4
5. 3
6. 11
7. 9
8. 3
9. 16 is less
10. 100

## Task 7a

1. 12
2. Nearer to 10
3. 24 hours
4. 13
5. 100
6. 8
7. 4 kg
8. 9
9. 2
10. 20

## Task 7b

1. A hexagon
2. Saturday
3. 3 coins
4. 12
5. cm (or inches)
6. 14
7. 4p
8. 14 books
9. 5 months
10. 5 triangles

## Task 7c

1. 4 tens (or 40)
2. 60
3. 7
4. Nearer to 20
5. 8
6. 10
7. Sat. and Sun.
8. 70
9. 14
10. 20

## Task 7d

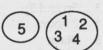

## Task 8a

1. Friday
2. 18 children
3. 4 corners
4. 10p, 5p, 5p
5. Nearer 1 kg
6. 2 halves
7. 8 and 13
8. 16
9. February
10. 4, 1

## Task 8b

## Task 8c

1. 8 o'clock
2. 7p change
3. kg (or lbs)
4. 12
5. 15
6. 19p
7. 6 chews
8. 5 pieces
9. 12 hours
10. One half

## Task 8d

Tom has 19 books.

## Task 9a

1. so = 12
2. do = 6
3. on + or = 18
4. ago = 12
5. Yes: odd = 7
6. sad = 11
7. Both equal 11
8. nor – add = 8
9. drag = 10
10. roars = 19

## Task 9b

1. 5
2. 50
3. 4
4. 11
5. 3
6. 33
7. 6
8. 14
9. 12
10. 15

## Task 9c

1. 3 hours
2. 5 sides
3. About 7 cm
4. Nearer to 10
5. A rectangle
6. 10p, 2p, 1p
7. 77, 76, 70, 67
8. 14 days
9. October
10. White

## Task 9d

1. 90
2. 11
3. 20
4. 8
5. 9
6. 12
7. 16
8. 19
9. 9
10. 9

## Task 10a

1. 12
2. 15
3. 5
4. 17
5. 9
6. 3
7. 16
8. 3
9. 30
10. 2

## Task 10b

| 1p | 3p | 2p |
|----|----|----|
| 3p | 2p | 1p |
| 2p | 1p | 3p |

or reflections
or rotations of this

## Task 10c

1. 60
2. 20
3. 11
4. 9
5. 21
6. 12
7. 18
8. 5
9. 24
10. 13

## Task 10d

1. Metres
2. 11 o'clock
3. An octagon
4. January
5. 2 boxes
6. 9 marbles
7. 5p, 2p, 2p, 1p
8. One quarter
9. Nearer 1 m
10. 6 rectangles

## Task 11a

1. Half past four
2. Monday
3. 6 sides
4. Autumn
5. 38p
6. 4 quarters
7. Metres (or ft)
8. A pentagon
9. 10 eggs
10. 5 people

## Task 11b

1. 80
2. 11
3. 14
4. 9
5. 7
6. 15
7. 15
8. 4
9. Ten 2p coins
10. 18

## Task 11c

1. 69
2. 17
3. 99
4. 8
5. 23
6. 15
7. 5
8. 20
9. 20
10. 2

## Task 11d

| 1 | 4 | 7 | 6 |
|---|---|---|---|
| 9 | | | 10 |
| 8 | 3 | 5 | 2 |

| 9 | 0 | 7 | 3 |
|---|---|---|---|
| 8 | | | 5 |
| 2 | 3 | 3 | 11 |

| 2 | 3 | 5 | 10 |
|---|---|---|---|
| 17 | | | 6 |
| 1 | 13 | 2 | 4 |

## Task 12a

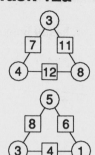

## Task 12b

1. Litres
2. 7 and 9
3. 07:30 (7:30 am)
4. November
5. 8 corners
6. Three quarters
7. 70
8. 5p, 5p, 5p
9. Nearer 30 kg
10. Friday

## Task 12c

1. Winter
2. 5 litres
3. A semi-circle
4. km or miles
5. 4
6. 102
7. 4 ropes
8. Two 5p coins
9. 6 birds
10. 6 squares

## Task 12d

a.
$5-4+3+2-1=5$
or
$5+4-3-2+1=5$

b.
$2+2-3+4-5=0$

## Task 13a

1. 8 catches
2. Peter
3. 11 catches
4. 14 catches
5. Peter
6. 7 catches
7. 12 catches
8. 11 catches
9. Ann
10. 8 more

## Task 13b

1. 23
2. 9 tens (or 90)
3. 14
4. 8
5. 16
6. One half
7. 20
8. 40
9. 18
10. 10p, 5p, 2p, 2p

## Task 13c

1. 1000 g in a kg
2. 3:30 (or 03.30)
3. 2 edges
4. 2 weeks
5. One half
6. Spring
7. 150
8. 20 cm short
9. 3
10. 13

## Task 13d

1. 90
2. – (minus)
3. 5
4. 80
5. 15
6. 6
7. 14
8. 34
9. 28
10. 1

## Task 14a

1. 5
2. 4
3. 2p
4. 6
5. 45
6. + (plus)
7. 16
8. 13
9. 48
10. 4 coins

## Task 14b

1. 12 marbles
2. 12 gloves
3. 3 packets
4. 40
5. 3 cakes each
6. 10p
7. A circle
8. 50 cm
9. 20
10. 20p

## Task 14c

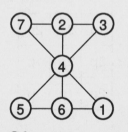

Other arrangements are possible.

## Task 14d

1. 14
2. 0
3. 4
4. 54
5. 101
6. × (times)
7. 8
8. 2
9. 1
10. 14

## Task 15a

1. 11
2. January
3. The triangle
4. Summer
5. 1000 ml in 1 l
6. About 20 kg
7. Two wholes
8. 4 coins
9. Midnight
10. One quarter

## Task 15b

1. 100
2. ÷ (divided by)
3. One whole
4. 11
5. 96
6. 24 is even
7. 30
8. 89
9. 3 and a half
10. 110

## Task 15c

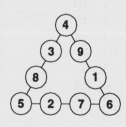

## Task 15d

1. One half
2. 10
3. 23
4. 50
5. 21 is odd
6. 0
7. 410
8. 8
9. 24
10. 54

## 8c

**1** What time does this clock show?  `08:00`

**2** Some nuts cost 13p. What is the change from 20p?

**3** What unit would you use to weigh a bag of potatoes?

**4** What is the total of 3 and 3 and 3 and 3?

**5** What number is half way between 10 and 20?

**6** How much is this altogether?

**7** Kevin and Sharon shared 12 chews equally.
How many did Sharon get?

**8** How many 4 cm pieces of tape can be cut from 20 cm?

**9** How many hours from midnight to noon?

**10** What fraction of these spots are ringed?

## 8d

Tom has fewer than 20 books.

He counted his books in fours. He had three left over.
He counted them in fives. He had four left over.

How many books does Tom have?

# Crack the code

D R A G O N S
**1 2 3 4 5 6 7**

Add up the numbers standing for the letters in each word.

1  Which is the greatest: **go**, **an** or **so**?

2  Which is the least: **on**, **as** or **do**?

3  What is the total of **on** and **or**?

4  Dragons lived long **ago**.  What is the value of **ago**?

5  Is **odd** an odd number?

6  Which is more: **dog** or **sad**?

7  Are these equal: **ran** and **gag**?

8  What is the difference between **add** and **nor**?

9  Which is less: **drag** or **door**?

10  A dragon **roars**. What is the total value of **roars**?

## 9b

| | | | |
|---|---|---|---|
| **1** | Subtract 7 from 12. | **6** | One more than 32. |
| **2** | $5 \times 10$. | **7** | $\square \times 2 = 12$. |
| **3** | $13 - 9$. | **8** | $8 + 6$. |
| **4** | 2 times 5, add 1. | **9** | Four threes. |
| **5** | $15 \div \square = 5$. | **10** | $2 + 8 + 5$. |

## 9c

**1** It is 09:00.
How long is it to noon?

**2** How many sides has a pentagon?

**3** Is your palm about 7 cm or 17 cm wide?

**4** Is 14 nearer to 10 or nearer to 20?

**5** What shape is a post-card?

**6** Which three coins make 13p?

**7** Put in order, biggest first: 67, 76, 77, 70.

**8** How many days in a fortnight?

**9** It is October.
What was 12 months ago?

**10** Is the centre bead black or white?

## 9d

| | | | |
|---|---|---|---|
| **1** | 10 times 9. | **6** | $20 - 8$. |
| **2** | $5 + 6$. | **7** | $\square \div 4 = 4$. |
| **3** | Five more than fifteen. | **8** | Multiply 9 by 2, then add 1. |
| **4** | $2 \times \square = 16$. | **9** | 8 plus 3 minus 2. |
| **5** | Subtract 8 from 17. | **10** | $2 + 3 + 4$. |

## 10a

1. $2 + 4 + 6$.
2. 20 take away 5.
3. $3 \times \square = 15$.
4. Add ten to seven.
5. Take 10 from 19.

6. How many 4s in 12?
7. $10 + 10 - 4$.
8. How many more than 6 is 9?
9. Subtract 1 from 31.
10. How many 10p coins make 20p?

## 10b

Draw a blank $3 \times 3$ grid.

This is your stamp card.

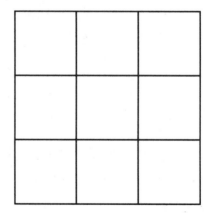

Imagine you have three 1p, three 2p and three 3p stamps.

One stamp must be stuck in each space on the card.

The total of each row, column and diagonal must be 6p.

Write the values of the stamps in the spaces.

1  $10 \times 6$.

2  12 more than 8.

3  $3 + 4 + 4$.

4  $\square \div 3 = 3$.

5  Five times four, plus one.

6  $\square + 6 = 18$.

7  Increase eight by ten.

8  Subtract 14 from 19.

9  What is next: 8, 12, 16, 20 …?

10  $20 - 7$.

1  What unit would you use to measure the width of a swimming pool?

2  It is 3 o'clock.  What time was it 4 hours ago?

3  What is this shape called?

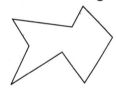

4  In which month is New Year's Day?

5  An egg box holds six eggs.
How many boxes are needed for 10 eggs?

6  Suzy had 18 marbles.  Milly had half as many.
How many did Milly have?

7  Which four coins make 10p?

8  What fraction of the large triangle is white?

9  Are you nearer 1 metre or 3 metres tall?

10  How many rectangles can you see altogether?

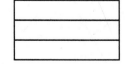

## 11a

1   What time does this clock show?    `04:30`

2   What is four days after Thursday?

3   How many sides has a hexagon?

4   In what season do leaves fall off trees?

5   How much is this?

6   How many quarters make one whole?

7   What unit would you use to measure the height of a tower?

8   What is this shape called?

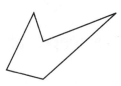

9   There are 20 eggs in my basket.
    One half of them are broken.  How many are whole?

10  There are 20 apples in a box,
    How many people can have 4 apples each?

## 11b

1   8 multiplied by 10.

2   Nine less than twenty.

3   6 + 8.

4   3 times 4, minus 3.

5   7 ÷ 1.

6   3 + 3 + 3 + 3 + 3.

7   5 + 2 + 8.

8   Divide 20 by 5.

9   How many 2p coins make 20p?

10  Find the sum of 11 and 7.

1. Write **sixty-nine** in figures.
2. $6 + 2 + 9$.
3. One less than 100.
4. $\square \div 8 = 1$.
5. $20 + 3$.
6. Seven plus eight.
7. From 15 take 10.
8. What is next: 60, 50, 40, 30 …?
9. $25 - 5$.
10. $\square \times 9 = 18$.

Copy and complete each diagram.

Make each side add to 18.

| 1 | 4 | 7 |   |
|---|---|---|---|
| 9 |   |   |   |
|   | 3 |   | 2 |

Make each side add to 19.

|   |   | 7 | 3 |
|---|---|---|---|
| 8 |   |   | 5 |
| 2 | 3 |   |   |

Make each side add to 20.

|   | 3 | 5 |   |
|---|---|---|---|
|   |   |   | 6 |
| 1 |   | 2 | 4 |

23

## 12a

Copy and complete each diagram.

A number in a square is the sum of the numbers on each side of it.

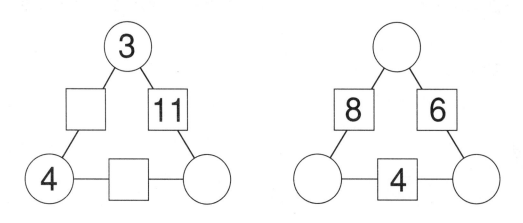

## 12b

1   What unit would you use to find how much a bucket holds?

2   Which two total sixteen: 6, 7, 8, 9?

3   It is 03:30. What time will it be in four hours' time?

4   In what month is Guy Fawkes Day?

5   How many corners has an octagon?

6   What fraction of the big triangle is shaded?

7   What is the value of 7 in 72?

8   Which three coins make 15p?

9   Is your weight nearer 30 kg or 130 kg?

10  It is Tuesday. What day was it four days ago?

1   In what season is it most likely to snow?

2   Does a large tin of paint hold 5 litres or 50 litres?

3   What is this shape called?

4   What unit would you use to measure the distance from London to Birmingham?

5   What number multiplied by itself gives 16?

6   Make the smallest whole number you can with these digits.

7   How many 3 m ropes can be cut from 12 m?

8   You have only 5p coins.
    How many should you use to pay for 2 chews at 3p each?

9   8 of the 14 birds sitting on a tree flew off.  How many were left?

10  How many squares can you see altogether?

**2d**

Copy and complete these to make each sum correct.
Each time put two + and two − signs instead of the boxes.

a.   5 ☐ 4 ☐ 3 ☐ 2 ☐ 1 = 5

b.   2 ☐ 2 ☐ 3 ☐ 4 ☐ 5 = 0

Some children tried to catch a ball.
They tried 10 times with each hand.

 right hand

 left hand

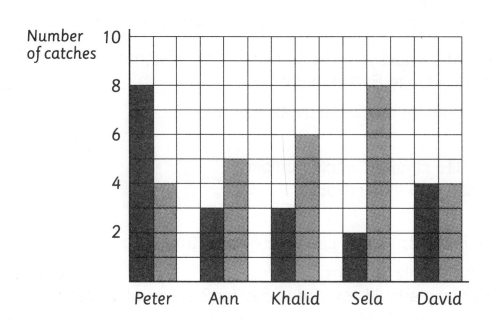

Number of catches

1 How many catches did David make with both hands?

2 Who caught the most balls with both hands?

3 How many right-hand catches did Khalid and Ann make together?

4 What was the total number of left-hand catches made by Sela, Peter and David?

5 Who is most likely to be left-handed?

6 How many more right-hand than left-hand catches did Sela make?

7 How many of his 20 catches did David drop?

8 How many catches did Khalid drop?

9 Who caught four fewer right-hand catches than Sela?

10 How many more right-hand than left-hand catches were there?

## 13b

1   13 + 10.

2   How many tens in 98?

3   3 + 5 + 6.

4   Take 12 from 20.

5   Add 9 to 7.

6   Which is greater: $\frac{1}{2}$ or $\frac{1}{4}$?

7   How many more than 10 is 30?

8   Round 38 to the nearest 10.

9   Two groups of nine.

10   Which four coins make 19p?

## 13c

1   How many grams in a kilogram?

2   It is 10:30. What time will it be in 5 hours' time?

3   How many edges has a semi-circle?

4   How many weeks in a fortnight?

5   What is one quarter plus one quarter?

6   In what season do daffodils bloom?

7   Write **one hundred and fifty** in figures.

8   By how much is 80 cm short of 1 metre?

9   Add 1 to the difference between 7 and 5.

10   What is two less than three fives?

## 13d

1   One more than 89.

2   If 4 = 7 ◆ 3, what is ◆?

3   2 + 3 + □ = 10.

4   40 + 40.

5   Add 8 to 7.

6   How many more than 14 is 20?

7   Two sevens.

8   24 + 10.

9   30 − 2.

10   8 + 2 − 9.

## 14a

1. $1 + \square + 2 = 8$.
2. $20 - 16$.
3. One quarter of 8p.
4. $5 - 3 + 4$.
5. $40 + 5$.
6. If $15 = 9 \blacklozenge 6$, what is $\blacklozenge$?
7. 15 take away 8, add 9.
8. Find the total of 4 and 9.
9. $58 - 10$.
10. How many 5p coins make 20p?

## 14b

1. Jason has 16 marbles. He loses 8, then wins 4.
   How many marbles has he now?

2. How many gloves in 6 pairs?

3. There are 5 sunflower seeds in a packet.
   I want to grow 12 sunflowers.
   How many packets should I buy?

4. What number is 10 times as big as 4?

5. 5 children shared 15 cakes equally between them.
   How many cakes did each one get?

6. 1 litre of milk costs 40p. What does one quarter of a litre cost?

7. What shape is the base of a tin of baked beans?

8. How many centimetres in half a metre?

9. What number is half way between 15 and 25?

10. Li has saved three 1p,
    one 2p and three 5p coins.
    How much has she saved altogether?

Copy the diagram.

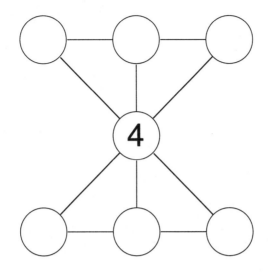

Use each of the numbers 1, 2, 3, 5, 6 and 7.
Write one number in every circle.

The sum of the three numbers in any straight line
must add up to 12.

1 2 3 and 5 6 7

4d

| | |
|---|---|
| **1** 8 plus 10 minus 4. | **6** If 12 = 6 ◆ 2, what is ◆? |
| **2** 0 × 6. | **7** What is next: 24, 20, 16, 12 …? |
| **3** ☐ + 5 + 8 = 17. | **8** 20 minus 18. |
| **4** 34 + 20. | **9** What is 1 times 1 times 1? |
| **5** One more than 100. | **10** 9 − 2 + 7. |

## 15a

1    To the difference between 13 and 5, add 3.

2    May is four months after which month?

3    Which has the smallest area,
   the square, the circle or the triangle?

4    What is usually the warmest season?

5    How many millilitres are there in a litre?

6    A family eats 5 kg of potatoes each week.
   About how many kg of potatoes will they eat in a month?

7    Two halves and four quarters make how many wholes?

8    What is the least number of coins needed to make 18p?

9    It is half past one at night.
   What time was it one and a half hours ago?

10   What fraction of these buttons
   are ringed?

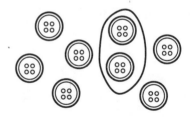

## 15b

1    10 mutiplied by itself.

2    If 9 = 18 ◆ 2, what is ◆?

3    Double one half.

4    12 minus 8, plus 7.

5    90 + 6.

6    Is 24 odd or even?

7    60 − 30.

8    One before 90.

9    One half of seven.

10   **One hundred and ten** in figures.

Copy the diagram.

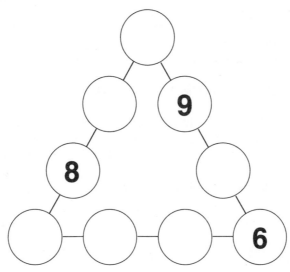

Write the numbers from 1 to 9 in the circles.
Three of the numbers are already in place.

The sum of the numbers on each side of the triangle
must add up to 20.

1 2 3 4 5 6 7 8 9

| | | | |
|---|---|---|---|
| **1** | One quarter of 2. | **6** | From the sum of 2 and 9 take 11. |
| **2** | 7 plus 8 minus 5. | **7** | **Four hundred and ten** in figures. |
| **3** | 30 – 7. | **8** | $2 \times 2 \times 2$. |
| **4** | Double 25. | **9** | Five fives, take away 1. |
| **5** | Is 21 odd or even? | **10** | 74 – 20. |

PUBLISHED BY THE PRESS SYNDICATE OF THE UNIVERSITY OF CAMBRIDGE
The Pitt Building, Trumpington Street, Cambridge CB2 1RP, United Kingdom

CAMBRIDGE UNIVERSITY PRESS
The Edinburgh Building, Cambridge CB2 2RU, United Kingdom
40 West 20th Street, New York, NY 10011-4211, USA
10 Stamford Road, Oakleigh, Melbourne 3166, Australia

This edition first published 1998

Printed in the United Kingdom by Scotprint Ltd, Musselburgh

A catalogue record for this book is available from the British Library

ISBN 0 521 65562 5 paperback

Cover Illustration by Tony Hall
Cartoons by Tim Sell